SCHOLASTIC
News
Nonfiction Readers®

Who Works at the White House?

By Marge Kennedy

Children's Press®
An Imprint of Scholastic Inc.
New York Toronto London Auckland Sydney
Mexico City New Delhi Hong Kong
Danbury, Connecticut

These content vocabulary word builders are for grades 1–2.

Subject Consultant: Eli J. Lesser, MA, Director of Education, National Constitution Center, Philadelphia, Pennsylvania

Reading Consultant: Cecilia Minden-Cupp, PhD, Early Literacy Consultant and Author, Chapel Hill, North Carolina

Photographs © 2009: Alamy Images/SHOUT: 4 bottom left, 12; AP Images: 11 (Manuel Balce Ceneta), 5 bottom right, 8 (Greg Gibson), 13 (Kenneth Lambert), 23 top left (Wilfredo Lee), 9 (Marcy Nighswander); Corbis Images: 4 top, 6, 7 top (Eric Draper/Reuters), 23 bottom right (Brooks Kraft), 23 bottom left (Wally McNamee); George Bush Presidential Library: back cover, 15; Getty Images: 17 top right (Mannie Garcia), cover, 5 top left, 14 (Mandel Ngan/AFP), 17 bottom left, 17 top left (Paul J. Richards/AFP), 4 bottom right, 5 top right, 16, 18 (Mark Wilson); Redux Pictures/Paul Hosefros/The New York Times: 5 bottom left, 10; Ronald Reagan Presidential Library: 1, 2, 17 bottom right, 19; The Image Works/John Nordell: 7 bottom; VEER: 20 bottom (Brand X Photography), 21 (Image Source Photography), 20 top (PhotoAlto Photography); White House Historical Association/Tina Hager: 23 top right.

Series Design: Simonsays Design!
Art Direction, Production, and Digital Imaging: Scholastic Classroom Magazines

Library of Congress Cataloging-in-Publication Data

Kennedy, Marge M., 1950-
Who Works at the White House? / Marge Kennedy.
    p. cm. – (Scholastic news nonfiction readers)
Includes bibliographical references and index.
ISBN 13: 978-0-531-21099-4 (lib. bdg.)   978-0-531-22435-9 (pbk.)
ISBN 10: 0-531-21099-5 (lib. bdg.)   0-531-22435-X (pbk.)
1. White House (Washington, D.C.)–Juvenile literature. 2. White House (Washington, D.C.)–Employees–Juvenile literature. 3. Presidents–United States–Juvenile literature. 4. Presidents–United States–Staff–Juvenile literature. 5. Washington (D.C.)–Buildings, structures, etc.–Juvenile literature. I. Title.
F204.W5K457 2009
975.3–dc22   2008037426

©2009 Scholastic Inc.
All rights reserved. Published in 2009 by Children's Press, an imprint of Scholastic Inc.
Published simultaneously in Canada. Printed in the United States of America.   44

SCHOLASTIC, CHILDREN'S PRESS, and associated logos are trademarks and/or registered trademarks of Scholastic Inc.
1 2 3 4 5 6 7 8 9 10 R 18 17 16 15 14 13 12 11 10 09

CONTENTS

WORD HUNT

Look for these words as you read. They will be in **bold**.

advisers
(ad-**vye**-zurz)

helicopter pilot
(**hel**-uh-kop-tur
pye-luht)

**housekeeping
staff**
(**houss**-kee-ping staf)

4

chef
(shef)

gardeners
(**gard**-uh-nurz)

photographer
(fuh-**tog**-ruh-fur)

Secret Service agents
(**see**-krit **sur**-viss **ay**-juhnts)

A Very Busy House!

The President has a big job. He doesn't do it alone! He has **advisers** to help him lead our country. Many other people work at the White House too.

advisers

Advisers help the President decide what is best for the United States.

WHITE HOUSE SITUATION ROOM

CL

Some people work to keep the President safe. **Secret Service agents** stay near him at all times. They go with the President when he travels.

Secret Service agents

Secret Service agents jogged with President Clinton.

A **photographer** goes almost everywhere with the President.

The photographer takes many photos every day. The photos help us know about a President's life.

photographer

A photographer followed President George W. Bush to take pictures of him.

The President travels often. A **helicopter pilot** flies him to and from the airport.

The helicopter takes off and lands on the White House lawn.

helicopter pilot

The helicopter that carries the President is called Marine One.

The main **chef** at the White House has a big job. She and her helpers cook for the President. They also cook for parties. As many as 1,000 people may come to a party. That's a lot of cooking!

chef

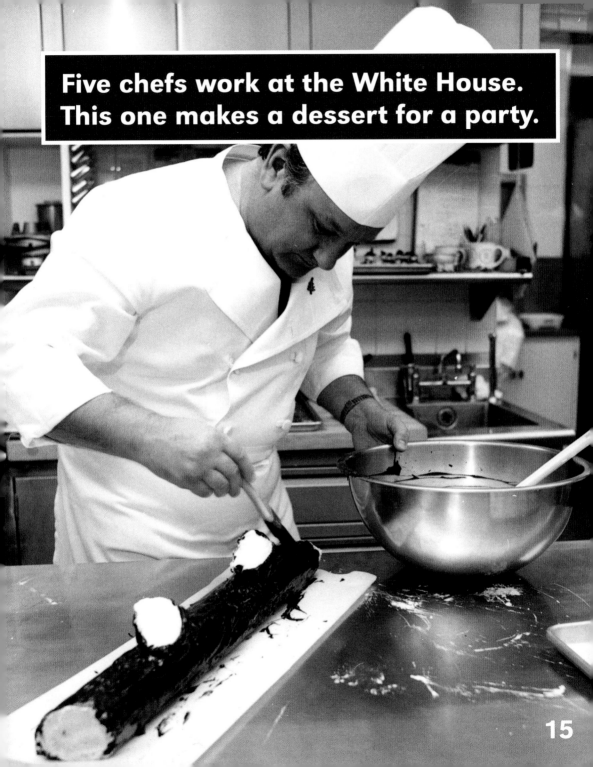

Five chefs work at the White House. This one makes a dessert for a party.

15

Did you know the White House has 132 rooms? The **housekeeping staff** keeps them all clean. They make sure the White House is ready for important guests.

housekeeping staff

17

Workers take care of the outside of the White House too. There are many plants and flowers in the gardens. **Gardeners** water them. They keep everything beautiful all year.

gardeners

About 12,000 tulips bloom in the White House gardens.

YOU CAN WRITE TO THE PRESIDENT!

One person's job at the White House is to help the President answer mail from kids. If you write to the President, you will get a letter back!

The President
of the United States
The White House
1600 Pennsylvania Ave., NW
Washington, D.C. 20500

● **Here is the President's address.
Don't forget the stamp!**

January 21, 2009

Grace Brown
123 First Street
Lexington, KY 40515

The President of the United States
The White House
1600 Pennsylvania Ave., NW
Washington, D.C. 20500

Dear Mr. President,

My name is Grace. I am 7 years old. I live in Kentucky.

Here is my question for you: What do you think kids can do to help our country?

Thank you for answering my letter.

Sincerely,
Grace Brown

Here's what to do:

● **Include your name and address so the President can write back to you!**

● **Begin your letter with "Dear Mr. President."**

● **Tell the President your age and where you live.**

● **Ask the President a question, or tell him your wish for America.**

YOUR NEW WORDS

advisers (ad-**vye**-zurz) people who give ideas or information to help other people

chef (shef) someone who cooks for others

gardeners (**gard**-uh-nurz) people who grow and care for flowers and other plants

helicopter pilot (**hel**-uh-kop-tur **pye**-luht) someone who flies an aircraft with large spinning blades on top

housekeeping staff (**houss**-kee-ping staf) a team of people who take care of a house

photographer (fuh-**tog**-ruh-fur) someone who takes pictures with a camera

Secret Service agents (**see**-krit **sur**-viss **ay**-juhnts) people whose job it is to keep the President and his family safe

FOUR MORE WHITE HOUSE JOBS

Guard
watches the building

Florist
decorates with flowers

Press Secretary
talks with reporters

Calligrapher
hand-writes beautiful cards

INDEX

FIND OUT MORE

Book:

Grace, Catherine, O. *The White House: An Illustrated History*. New York: Scholastic Nonfiction, 2003.

Website:

The White House Historical Association
www.whitehousehistory.org/06/subs/06_c.html

MEET THE AUTHOR

Marge Kennedy worked as a volunteer for one of the Presidents—John F. Kennedy—when she was 10.